26 WEEK DEVOTIONAL
NAL

MW00617703

PRAYER

APPROACHING THE
THRONE OF GRACE

A Devotable Compilation Project

Table of Contents

Prayer

What is prayer? How are we supposed to pray? How often should we pray? How long are our prayers supposed to be?

These are questions everyone asks at one time or another. Prayer is how we communicate with our Father. It is our conversation with God Himself. Prayer is a vital piece to a meaningful and purpose-driven Christian life.

However, not everyone grows up knowing how to pray or has had good teaching on how to use the power of prayer in their everyday life. This devotional and prayer journal aims to do those two things; teach people how to pray and show them the power of prayer.

Our goal with this devotional is to help you understand what prayer is and to teach you the vital skills needed to have a meaningful prayer life. We also want to encourage you to write about your prayers, your day, your needs, and more. Journaling your prayer life is an important way to see how your prayers are answered and rejoice when that happens.

Use this devotional and journal to assist you in cultivating a life of perpetual prayer and journal your experiences as they happen. When you do, you'll be able to look back and recognize all that God has and is doing for you each day.

How to Use This Journal

Each week starts with a devotional about prayer. Read the devotional and accompanying Scripture to learn and deepen your knowledge of what prayer is.

Each day of the week, there are questions relating to that week's devotional. Some questions might ask you to reflect on your life and how you can improve an aspect of your prayer time. Some questions might lead you to learn how to become a more effective prayer warrior.

Whatever the case is, answer each question with the intent of learning and improving your prayer life.

Lastly, there are repetitive questions each day that everyone should be able to ask and answer relating to their prayers. Journal about prayer requests that are heavy on your soul, write and rejoice about requests that have been answered, and confess things you need to deal with.

As you continue with the journal, you'll be able to look back at the previous pages and see how things you were once praying about have been fulfilled. You'll get a better sense of how God is working through your life and how He is answering your prayers. Often we pray for something and forget about it several weeks down the road. Journaling these things helps us remember just how good God is to always answer our prayers.

Week 1

What is Prayer?

Pray constantly.
1 Thessalonians 5:17

Have you ever struggled with prayer? For me, I worry about my posture, my speech, where to pray, when to pray. I feel as if my prayers should be these elegant, colorful, long, and mountain moving speeches.

Instead, my prayers often sound like this: "God, please help me." "God, where did I place my keys?" "God, I just need You today." I hear the prayers of others that are beautiful, long, seemingly flowing with ease, and I think to myself, *"Man, I wish I could pray like that!"* Sometimes I stop praying because I don't always pray with ease or have a hard time coming up with what to say.

Sound familiar?

God in His grace and mercy has shown me that I should not compare my prayers with others or overthink prayer. So let's break it down to basics. What exactly is prayer?

Prayer, defined by Merriam Webster is, "an address (such as a petition) to God or a god in word or thought." Simply put, prayer is a conversation with God. Since God longs to communicate with us, He

gives us several verses in Matthew regarding prayer as a blueprint for how to pray. "Therefore, you should pray like this: Our Father in heaven, Your name be honored as holy. Your kingdom come. Your will be done on earth as it is in heaven. Give us today our daily bread. And forgive us our debts, as we also have forgiven our debtors. And do not bring us into temptation, but deliver us from the evil one. For Yours is the kingdom and the power and the glory forever. Amen." (Matthew 6:9-13)

He also gives us instructions on how not to pray, "Whenever you pray, you must not be like the hypocrites, because they love to pray standing in the synagogues and on the street corners to be seen by people. I assure you: They've got their reward! ... When you pray, don't babble like the idolaters, since they imagine they'll be heard for their many words. Don't be like them, because your Father knows the things you need before you ask Him." (Matthew 6:5, 7-8)

God loves to communicate with us no matter how small, brief, or simple our prayers are. Prayer is a gift God gave us to communicate with Him. Isn't that beautiful?

God, thank You that You bend Your ear to earth just to hear us. Thank You for Your unconditional love for us and longing to have a relationship with us. God, thank You for the gift of prayer. May we not compare ourselves to others when we pray and recognize that prayer is a special connection just between us. Thank You for providing Your Word as a guide on how to pray.

Written by Alexis M. Newlin

Day One

How have you struggled with prayer in the past?

Today I praise God for...

Today I am confessing...

Today I am praying for...

My reflections...

Day Two

What Bible verses help you understand prayer?

Today I praise God for...

Today I am confessing...

Today I am praying for...

My reflections...

Day Three

How do you prefer to pray?

_____

_____

_____

Today I praise God for...

_____

_____

Today I am confessing...

_____

_____

Today I am praying for...

_____

_____

My reflections...

_____

_____

Day Four

What is your biggest hindrance to prayer?

Today I praise God for...

Today I am confessing...

Today I am praying for...

My reflections...

Day Five

What is your personal definition of prayer?

_____

_____

_____

Today I praise God for...

_____

_____

Today I am confessing...

_____

_____

Today I am praying for...

_____

_____

My reflections...

_____

_____

Day Six

Would you be willing to try another style of prayer?

_____

Today I praise God for...

_____

Today I am confessing...

_____

Today I am praying for...

_____

My reflections...

_____

Day Seven

Have you ever journaled your prayers? Commit to journaling at least one prayer this week.

Today I praise God for...

Today I am confessing...

Today I am praying for...

My reflections...

18

Pray at all times in the Spirit with every prayer and request, and stay alert in this with all perseverance and intercession for all the saints.

Ephesians 6:18

Week 2

I Don't Feel Like Praying

The Lord answered her, "Martha, Martha, you are worried and upset about many things, but one thing is necessary." Mary has made the right choice, and it will not be taken away from her.'
Luke 10:41-42

Maybe it's just me, but sometimes I don't feel like praying. Isn't that bad for me to say? Prayer is such a beautiful experience. To be humble before God and spend intimate time with Him is irreplaceable and completely necessary. Yet, I'm here admitting that sometimes I don't feel like praying.

Sometimes there is just too much work to do, and I don't feel as if I can do both. Lessons need planning. Dinner needs cooking. The house needs cleaning. Life is messy. I don't feel like I have time to pray when so much needs to be done.

Then I'm reminded of someone else who had so much to do. She was busy. She was so busy preparing for Jesus that she didn't have time to pause and be with Jesus. In the busyness of life, she neglected to slow down and spend time with her Savior. Dare I say we all have a little bit

of Martha in us? We all get in a hurry. We all get too busy. We sometimes don't feel like being still with God because we don't think we have the time. But today God wants all of us to remember a few simple things:

Prayer strengthens us (Luke 22:43-44). When we least feel like praying is when we most need it (1 Peter 5:7). When we don't take time to pray, we become easy prey (1 Peter 5:8). Jesus prayed, therefore we certainly need to pray (Luke 6:12; Matthew 14:23). Prayer is communication with God (Matthew 6:6-13).

All in all, when I am humbled before God, I am recharged. He wants to be in communication with me, regardless of my circumstances. One of the best parts about prayer is that when I don't feel like praying, but do, I can't stop praying.

Prayer isn't an obligation, it's a privilege. Prayer isn't about whether I feel like it. In turn, prayer gives the power I was needing, the answer I was waiting on, and the guidance I was hoping for.

God, I pray that we never allow the busyness of life to affect our relationship with You. May we never allow the gift of life, to get in the way of the relationship with the Giver. Thank You for being patient with us when we do and getting us on the right track when we stray. In Jesus' name, Amen.

Written by Chanel Moore

Day One

How do you become distracted in life?

_____

_____

_____

Today I praise God for...

_____

_____

Today I am confessing...

_____

_____

Today I am praying for...

_____

_____

My reflections...

_____

_____

Day Two

Do you ever feel there are so many distractions that it's hard to focus on a relationship with God?

Today I praise God for...

Today I am confessing...

Today I am praying for...

My reflections...

Day Three

Do you feel like the blessings of life seem more like curses when it comes to time management?

_____

_____

_____

Today I praise God for...

_____

_____

Today I am confessing...

_____

_____

Today I am praying for...

_____

_____

My reflections...

_____

_____

Day Four

How can you manage time better?

Today I praise God for...

Today I am confessing...

Today I am praying for...

My reflections...

Day Five

Do you think the distractions of life keep you from a deeper prayer life?

Today I praise God for...

Today I am confessing...

Today I am praying for...

My reflections...

Day Six

Have you prayed when you didn't feel like it and felt a breakthrough?

_____

_____

Today I praise God for...

_____

Today I am confessing...

_____

Today I am praying for...

_____

My reflections...

_____

Day Seven

Do you think God has a deeper prayer life ready for you with proper management of time, with Him as number one?

Today I praise God for...

Today I am confessing...

Today I am praying for...

My reflections...

Subscribe to our email list for
more daily devotions at
devotableapp.com/subscribe

Rejoice in hope; be patient in affliction; be persistent in prayer.
Romans 12:12

Week 3

Father, Forgive Them

Then Jesus said, "Father, forgive them, because they do not know what they are doing."
Luke 23:34

Have you ever considered the words you will speak in your final moments of life? What will you wish to communicate to your family and friends? What will you say to those who have hurt you? Will you speak words that wound or words that give life?

The Gospels record seven statements spoken by Jesus from the cross, the first of which is, "Father, forgive them because they do not know what they are doing" (Luke 23:34). With this simple prayer, Jesus spoke life-filled words of compassion and mercy, of healing and reconciliation. Even as His body hung, broken on a Roman cross, Jesus' heart was intentionally focused on others.

Consider all that Jesus was going through during His crucifixion: the loneliness, the embarrassment, the temptation to quit. Each of these paled in comparison to the unbearable physical agony of suffering the brutality of the cross. Yet, Jesus had the courage and conviction to call upon His Father to extend forgiveness.

Jesus understood the significance of His mission, and He focused His prayer on the people for whom He was dying.

Jesus had every right to call down the wrath of God upon all mankind, but He used His words instead to express unconditional love. Jesus could have summoned legions of angels to avenge Him, yet He called upon His Father to forgive those who crucified Him. Jesus could have stepped down from the cross and taught the scoffers there a lesson in justice, but He hung on the cross and taught them a lesson in grace. Jesus understood the importance of final words, of final lessons.

Jesus prayed for those in the shadow of the cross. He prayed for each of us as well. The apostle Paul said that, "...all have sinned and fall short of the glory of God" (Romans 3:23). There is not a person in all of creation that measures up to God's righteous demands. Furthermore, our sin carries with it an infinite debt. Paul wrote, "...the wages of sin is death..." (Romans 6:23). For us, this death is not only physical, but spiritual, and, if not for the sacrifice of the Messiah, we would be forever lost in our sins.

Jesus prayed on our behalf during His final moments of life. We, too, should pray for one another. May our words always be filled with compassion as we reflect on Jesus' life-giving prayer from the cross.

Lord Jesus, thank You for dying on the cross for the forgiveness of my sins. Help me to always offer words of life, even in difficult circumstances. In Your holy name I pray, Amen.

Written by Chuck Kralik

Day One

To whom do you think Jesus was referring when He said, "Father, forgive them?"

_____

_____

_____

Today I praise God for...

_____

_____

Today I am confessing...

_____

_____

Today I am praying for...

_____

_____

My reflections...

_____

_____

Day Two

What do you think Jesus meant by saying, "...they do not know what they are doing?"

_____

_____

_____

Today I praise God for...

_____

_____

Today I am confessing...

_____

_____

Today I am praying for...

_____

_____

My reflections...

_____

_____

Day Three

What do Jesus' words teach us about forgiving others?

_____

_____

_____

Today I praise God for...

_____

_____

Today I am confessing...

_____

_____

Today I am praying for...

_____

_____

My reflections...

_____

_____

Day Four

What do Jesus' words teach us about forgiving ourselves?

Today I praise God for...

Today I am confessing...

Today I am praying for...

My reflections...

Day Five

This is one of Jesus' seven recorded statements from the cross. What other things did Jesus say from the cross?

Today I praise God for...

Today I am confessing...

Today I am praying for...

My reflections...

Day Six

Which of Jesus' seven statements is most meaningful to you?

Today I praise God for...

Today I am confessing...

Today I am praying for...

My reflections...

Day Seven

What does Jesus' death on the cross mean for you?

_____

_____

_____

Today I praise God for...

_____

_____

Today I am confessing...

_____

_____

Today I am praying for...

_____

_____

My reflections...

_____

_____

Therefore, I want the men in every place to pray, lifting up holy hands without anger or argument.
1 Timothy 2:8

Week 4

How Then Should We Pray?

And I pray this: that your love will keep on growing in knowledge and every kind of discernment, so that you can approve the things that are superior and can be pure and blameless in the day of Christ, filled with the fruit of righteousness that comes through Jesus Christ to the glory and praise of God.
Philippians 1:9-11

In this passage, Paul begins his letter to the church of Philippi with a prayer. Now, this is not your typical Sunday morning small group prayer. Rather than praying for safe travels, the health of a fellow believer's cat, or the infamous "unspoken," Paul prays in a way that is both selfless and keenly biblical. He prays for the Philippian believers' spiritual growth, and in doing this he models for us what our prayers should look like. His prayer is especially striking as Paul is writing this letter from a Roman prison cell. Instead of asking for prayer for his deliverance, he prays for the growth and the example of Paul's prayer should revolutionize the way we pray for one another, especially for those in our churches.

Paul prays specifically for four results in the lives of the Philippian believers. He prays that the Philippians would grow in love through knowledge, that they would live a life of maturity and discernment, that they would be found pure and blameless at the return of Christ, and that their lives would be marked by the fruit of righteousness that comes from being in a relationship with Jesus. In a nutshell, Paul prays for their spiritual growth with the end in mind. His desire is to see believers grow and live up to their full potential so that when they stand before God, they would be found to have lived a life pleasing to Him.

Likewise, our prayers should be the same. We must pray selflessly, even in difficult circumstances, for the spiritual well-being of those in our churches. This week set out to pray that those in your church would grow in love and maturity, that they might be found pure and blameless at the return of Christ, having lived a life marked by the fruit of righteousness.

Lord, right now I want to lift up my brothers and sisters in Christ to You. I pray that their love for You and for others would abound in their knowledge of You. May they grow to be mature believers, so that at Your return they would be found blameless in Your sight. I also ask that You would enable them to live a life that bears fruit for Your glory. Amen.

Written by Corbin Charles Henderson

Day One

What are some examples of spiritually shallow or selfish prayers?

Today I praise God for...

Today I am confessing...

Today I am praying for...

My reflections...

Day Two

How does knowing Paul's circumstance change how you think about prayer?

Today I praise God for...

Today I am confessing...

Today I am praying for...

My reflections...

Day Three

Who can you pray for this week? Write out a list of at least five people.

Today I praise God for...

Today I am confessing...

Today I am praying for...

My reflections...

Day Four

How is growth in love connected to knowledge and discernment?

_____

_____

_____

Today I praise God for...

_____

_____

Today I am confessing...

_____

_____

Today I am praying for...

_____

_____

My reflections...

_____

_____

Day Five

Why is praying for the growth of others important for church growth and health?

Today I praise God for...

Today I am confessing...

Today I am praying for...

My reflections...

Day Six

How should knowing that Christ will someday return change how you pray for people?

Today I praise God for...

Today I am confessing...

Today I am praying for...

My reflections...

Day Seven

How does praying for others' spiritual growth glorify God?

Today I praise God for...

Today I am confessing...

Today I am praying for...

My reflections...

Listen to all of our devotions
on our podcast at
devotableapp.com/podcast

Therefore, confess your sins to one another and pray for one another, so that you may be healed. The urgent request of a righteous person is very powerful in its effect.

James 5:16

Week 5

Cultivating a Lifestyle of Prayer

Trust in Him at all times, you people; pour out your hearts before Him. God is our refuge. Selah.
Psalm 62:8

I don't know about you, but sometimes I allow my prayer times to become hurried and rushed as I try to pray on the run; or when I am trying to handle a problem on my own. As a result, I still feel rushed and anxious after the 'amen' because my focus was neither on God nor the prayer. It was on the problem and how I am going to handle it.

It is assumed David wrote Psalms 61, 62, & 63 during a time of refuge. Perhaps when he escaped during Absalom's rebellion or when he was hiding in the wilderness after Saul tried to kill him. Regardless, it is obvious David was dealing with anxiety and big problems. But David didn't leave God out; he shows us how to trust God, praise God, and pray to God in all circumstances.

In 1 Thessalonians, Paul reminds us to cultivate an attitude of prayer by praying continuously throughout our days. But sometimes I forget that God also wants me to come before Him in reverent, bold prayer.

God wants me to humble myself before Him, confess my sins, and reveal my deepest needs and desires.God wants my worship through prayer. God wants to renew my spirit, refresh my soul, and restore my faith. For me, that means getting up earlier, or even having my time with God before I get out of bed. The outcome of my day depends on whether I start my day with God or not. My attitude toward everything that day depends on my morning prayer time with God. On the days I skip time with God, I realize my focus is easily manipulated by the enemy.

There is not a single right or wrong way of spending time with God. Your time with God will be different than my time with God, as it should be. Our prayer times are the most important conversations of our days. Maybe we should pencil in 'prayer time' on our calendars if it will help us keep our date with God!

May you find peace and joy in the Lord today.

Thank You, Father, for your blessings on me. I come to You in bold praise and repentance. You are my refuge, my strength, and my all. Please forgive me for my rushed and mindless jabbering. Help me to be still in Your presence and pour out my heart before You. In Jesus' name, Amen.

Written by Crystal A. Dixon

Day One

Do you need to cultivate a lifestyle of prayer?

Today I praise God for...

Today I am confessing...

Today I am praying for...

My reflections...

Day Two

How can you prepare your heart and mind before you come to God?

Today I praise God for...

Today I am confessing...

Today I am praying for...

My reflections...

Day Three

In what ways can you incorporate worship into your prayer life?

_____

_____

_____

Today I praise God for...

_____

_____

Today I am confessing...

_____

_____

Today I am praying for...

_____

_____

My reflections...

_____

_____

Day Four

How can you improve your daily prayer time schedule?

Today I praise God for...

Today I am confessing...

Today I am praying for...

My reflections...

Day Five

Do you have specific times or days designated to pray for specific concerns, people, or situations?

Today I praise God for...

Today I am confessing...

Today I am praying for...

My reflections...

Day Six

Do you feel prayer journals or prayer lists can help you better organize your prayer time?

Today I praise God for...

Today I am confessing...

Today I am praying for...

My reflections...

Day Seven

What one specific aspect in your life must be adjusted so you can meet God in bold prayer and worship every day?

Today I praise God for...

Today I am confessing...

Today I am praying for...

My reflections...

Rejoice always! Pray constantly. Give thanks in everything, for this is God's will for you in Christ Jesus.

1 Thessalonians 5:16-18

Week 6

Pray Constantly

I have spoken these things to you while I remain with you. But the Counselor, the Holy Spirit—the Father will send Him in My name—will teach you all things and remind you of everything I have told you.
John 14:25-26

A relationship cannot be based on knowing about someone but must be based on truly knowing them. For example, I can tell you about my son, Cody, who passed away in 2007, but from my description, you cannot tell me about the lilt in his laugh or the unique way he told jokes. You can know some things about him, but you cannot know him or have a relationship with him. The same thing is true of Jesus. You must know Jesus intimately in order to have a relationship with Him. Knowing Jesus requires communication.

Prayer is our way of communicating with Jesus. It is a two-way conversation, involving both sharing and listening so we know one another. Paul taught us to, "Pray constantly" (I Thessalonians 5:17).

Because His Spirit is always with us, we can always speak and listen to Him.

Jesus tells us the Holy Spirit communicates with us. In John 14:18, Jesus promises His disciples He wouldn't leave them as orphans, and He continues in verses 25-26 saying, "I have spoken these things to you while I remain with you. But the Counselor, the Holy Spirit—the Father will send Him in My name—will teach you all things and remind you of everything I have told you." Again, in John 16:13 Jesus said, "When the Spirit of truth comes, He will guide you into all the truth."

If Cody was still here with me, I would constantly talk with him, and I would listen to him when he talked to me. In the same way, an intimate and loving relationship with Jesus means talking to Him about anything and everything, all the time, and listening for His responses. This is praying constantly. Constant prayer allows us to keep our connection with Him vibrant and meaningful and helps us to know Him better.

I choose to include Jesus in each and every aspect of my life in order to receive guidance. I also want to share myself as He shares Himself with me. I want to be with Him, receiving His love and giving my love in return. When Paul instructs us, "Pray constantly," he is saying, "Talk to Jesus and listen to Him about everything in your life." I encourage you to deepen and strengthen your relationship with Jesus by speaking and listening to Him constantly.

Lord, help me to remember Your constant presence with me. Give me eyes to see You, ears to hear You, and a heart to know You deeply. Amen.

Written by Donna E. Lane

Day One

What elements make for a deep and meaningful relationship?

_____

_____

_____

Today I praise God for...

_____

_____

Today I am confessing...

_____

_____

Today I am praying for...

_____

_____

My reflections...

_____

_____

Day Two

What are some ways you can move beyond knowledge about Jesus to truly knowing Him?

Today I praise God for...

Today I am confessing...

Today I am praying for...

My reflections...

Day Three

In what ways are you aware of His constant, loving presence with you right now?

Today I praise God for...

Today I am confessing...

Today I am praying for...

My reflections...

Day Four

What does it look like for the Holy Spirit to teach you all things and guide you into all truth?

Today I praise God for...

Today I am confessing...

Today I am praying for...

My reflections...

Day Five

How could you include Jesus in each and every aspect of your life?

Today I praise God for...

Today I am confessing...

Today I am praying for...

My reflections...

Day Six

In John 10:3-4, Jesus said, "The sheep hear his voice...the sheep follow him because they recognize his voice." What helps you recognize the voice of your Shepherd?

Today I praise God for...

Today I am confessing...

Today I am praying for...

My reflections...

Day Seven

What are some topics about which you would like to hear from Jesus? For each topic, take a few minutes to quiet your mind and listen for His responses to your question or conversation.

Today I praise God for...

Today I am confessing...

Today I am praying for...

My reflections...

Read and discover more free
devotions at
devotableapp.com

Therefore let us approach the throne of grace with boldness, so that we may receive mercy and find grace to help us at the proper time.

Hebrews 4:16

Week 7

Remember Me

Then Hezekiah turned his face to the wall and prayed to the Lord, 'Please Lord, remember how I have walked before You faithfully and wholeheartedly and have done what pleases You.' And Hezekiah wept bitterly. 2 Kings 20:2-3

I reference this passage in 2 Kings when life is at its lowest. It's the story of King Hezekiah and the report given to him from the prophet Isaiah. "This is what the Lord says: Put your house in order, because you are going to die; you will not recover." (2 Kings 20:1)

How do you pray when you've been given a bad report? When you look at your life and the only consistencies are terrible events beyond your control, there is a prayer you can utilize, and it starts with two words; "Remember me." If we're honest, tough times often cause us to feel like we're forgotten by God. Thankfully, God is very clear on how He feels about us. He loves us!

Tough times and extenuating circumstances can make us feel

like God is distant. The truth is He is with us and is aware of what's going on. Before reading this passage, I didn't know we could do such a thing! Desperate times call for desperate measures, right? Even if you can't state like Hezekiah that you've "walked faithfully", you still have the opportunity to pray and ask God to remember you.

Update the text for your situation. "Prepare your will, you're not going to survive this." "Start packing your things, the foreclosure is final." "Clean out your desk, we're downsizing." With every report given to us we can cry out to God and ask Him to remember us.

This year I've cried often. I couldn't understand why my husband and I were going through so much! I can relate to Hezekiah, because I cried bitterly as well. I know now that circumstances test our faith and build character. God is looking for our response to the tough times. Is she going to complain and curse? Is he going to abandon his faith? Because of what King Hezekiah prayed, God's report changed. "This is what the Lord God of your ancestor David says: I have heard your prayer; I have seen your tears. Look, I will heal you."(2 Kings 20:5b)

God heard King Hezekiah's prayer, and He'll hear yours.

Dear Lord, I acknowledge You as my Lord and Savior. I know what the report says, but am asking You to remember me, just as You heard and remembered the prayer of King Hezekiah. Help me not to allow difficult times to taint my vision of You and what You're doing in my life. I know You don't make mistakes. Please help me trust You. Thank You, in Jesus name I pray, Amen.

Written by Fiona "Fee" Williams

Day One

What tough situations are you currently dealing with that seem to have no resolve?

_____

_____

_____

Today I praise God for...

_____

_____

Today I am confessing...

_____

_____

Today I am praying for...

_____

_____

My reflections...

_____

_____

Day Two

How do you respond to bad news?

Today I praise God for...

Today I am confessing...

Today I am praying for...

My reflections...

Day Three

How often do you submit your concerns to God first, as opposed to complaining?

Today I praise God for...

Today I am confessing...

Today I am praying for...

My reflections...

Day Four

What do you pray about the most?

Today I praise God for...

Today I am confessing...

Today I am praying for...

My reflections...

Day Five

How do you combat emotional responses during trying times?

Today I praise God for...

Today I am confessing...

Today I am praying for...

My reflections...

Day Six

What did you take from King Hezekiah's prayer?

Today I praise God for...

Today I am confessing...

Today I am praying for...

My reflections...

Day Seven

How will your prayer life change after reading this devotional?

_____

_____

_____

Today I praise God for...

_____

_____

Today I am confessing...

_____

_____

Today I am praying for...

_____

_____

My reflections...

_____

_____

If we confess our sins, He is faithful and righteous to forgive us our sins and to cleanse us from all unrighteousness.
1 John 1:9

Week 8

So the World May Know

I am in them and You are in Me. May they be made completely one, so the world may know You have sent Me and have loved them as You have loved Me.
John 17:23

The phone call was years ago, but I remember the response to my unvoiced, "What now?" question as if it were yesterday. My husband and I had just been informed that staff members at our church stepped down from their positions because of improper conduct. Before I had the opportunity to ask my "What now?" question, the caller who notified us encouragingly explained that instead of dwelling on disappointment, the church leadership decided to pursue a prayerful plan of peace. Our church family had resolved to move forward together as one.

When we read the words of Jesus' prayer in John 17, we learn how important it is for us to live as one. In verse 23, Jesus requested, "May they be made completely one, so the world may know You have sent Me and have loved them as You have loved Me." When Christians are unified, it allows the world to see that God sent Jesus to be the

embodiment of life-changing love.

It is important to note that being "completely one" does not mean compromising our beliefs or nodding our heads in fake agreement with theology that is contrary to Biblical truth. When differences begin to divide, we should instead hone in on the similarities that initiate healing. For example, all believers are loved beyond measure by the same God. All believers have been assigned the same task of using our God-given gifts to glorify Him. All believers have been given the same forgiveness through Jesus' death and resurrection. All believers have access to the same Holy Spirit from whom we receive comfort and wisdom. "Being completely one," concentrates on these vital similarities. It allows peace to rule our hearts and our relationships, and it gives the world a wonderful glimpse of the love the Prince of Peace has for us. When onlookers had the opportunity to watch our church family respond to adversity in a spirit of unity, they witnessed that love in action.

It is humbling when we realize Jesus prayed not only for the people on the earth at that time, but for future believers as well. When my church family faced potential upheaval, we were already covered by our Savior's impassioned prayers. What a blessing to realize that when we pray for and actively pursue unity, we show others what true love is!

Lord, may I be faithful in praying for and actively working toward unified relationships with fellow Christians. Help me to live a life that exemplifies and emphasizes unity with other believers, so the world may experience Your love. Amen.

Written by Gwen Thielges

Day One

How does it make you feel to know that Jesus prayed for all believers ,
those who were alive then and those not yet born?

Today I praise God for...

Today I am confessing...

Today I am praying for...

My reflections...

Day Two

Can you recall instances when it has been difficult to live in unity with other Christians?

Today I praise God for...

Today I am confessing...

Today I am praying for...

My reflections...

Day Three

Is there a relationship in your life that would benefit from you intentionally praying for unity?

Today I praise God for...

Today I am confessing...

Today I am praying for...

My reflections...

Day Four

What has the Holy Spirit said to you about that relationship? Do you perhaps to forgive, a confession, or jealousy to eliminate?

Today I praise God for...

Today I am confessing...

Today I am praying for...

My reflections...

Day Five

Hebrews 5:7 reveals the passion with which Jesus prayed when it says, "...He offered prayers and appeals with loud cries and tears..." Do your prayers match that same passion?

Today I praise God for...

Today I am confessing...

Today I am praying for...

My reflections...

Day Six

How would your prayer life change if you prayed for unity among believers as Jesus did?

Today I praise God for...

Today I am confessing...

Today I am praying for...

My reflections...

Day Seven

What evidence is there of Christ's love growing in your life after praying for unity?

_____

_____

_____

Today I praise God for...

_____

_____

Today I am confessing...

_____

_____

Today I am praying for...

_____

_____

My reflections...

_____

_____

Support us or partner with us
as we try to reach more people
with the Gospel at
devotableapp.com/contribute

May my prayer be set before You as incense, the raising of my hands as the evening offering.
Psalm 141:2

Week 9

Praying for Wisdom

Now if any of you lacks wisdom, he should ask God, who gives to all generously and without criticizing, and it will be given to him. But let him ask in faith without doubting. For the doubter is like the surging sea, driven and tossed by the wind.
James 1:5-6

Today there are people all over the world asking questions. What job should I take? How do I resolve this conflict? Asking questions in a life with so many complex variables, personalities, and decisions to make is no challenge. Answering these questions, on the other hand, proves to be a trying and often wearisome task for many—if not all. When the pressures of life arise, where do we turn for answers in the fog that is life?

Consider places you might turn when these situations come about—a parent, sibling, or close friend? Possibly you turn to Google in search of reviews, statistics, or other avenues. For some, answers lie within a drug or addiction. With so many places to turn, how can a

person possibly know where to go when such critical questions need answers?

There is hope for the believer. James wrote concerning this very thing to Jewish believers who were under immense persecution. These hurting people were forced out of their hometowns and risked losing their lives. Fortunately, this was not a secret for the Jews alone, but it is true for believers even today!

First, when we are under any amount of pressure, it is God we must turn to. Although these questions may look different throughout each stage of a person's life, the answer remains the same—turn to God. Wisdom is not a quick answer or a piece of information; it is the truth of God's Word understood and applied. This is a call for every believer.

We Christ-followers are not merely commanded to ask for wisdom, but we are to do so without doubting. How often do we say a prayer, only to go about the rest of our day expecting nothing? To ask for wisdom with a doubt-filled heart is as ineffective as mopping up the water from the floor as rain pours in through an open window, rather than simply closing the window. Not only is this exhausting and frustrating—it is messy. This is what the life of the doubting believer looks like—the embodiment of the double-minded or indecisive man that James refers to. Christian, trade your doubts in for faith, trusting in the Word of God to supply all the wisdom you need for life and godliness.

Lord, thank You for Your providence in granting us wisdom when we need it. Forgive me for doubting You, and show me areas where I live with a double mind. Please give me wisdom in the midst of my circumstances. Amen.

Written by J. Heaven Henderson

Day One

How should this passage change our view of prayer?

_____

_____

_____

Today I praise God for...

_____

_____

Today I am confessing...

_____

_____

Today I am praying for...

_____

_____

My reflections...

_____

_____

Day Two

How does a prayer-filled response to pressures contrast a typical response in today's culture?

Today I praise God for...

Today I am confessing...

Today I am praying for...

My reflections...

Day Three

What can we learn about God's character from this passage?

_____

_____

_____

Today I praise God for...

_____

_____

Today I am confessing...

_____

_____

Today I am praying for...

_____

_____

My reflections...

_____

_____

Day Four

How are you tempted to seek the world's wisdom over the Lord's wisdom?

Today I praise God for...

Today I am confessing...

Today I am praying for...

My reflections...

Day Five

What are common doubts believers face today?

_____

_____

_____

Today I praise God for...

_____

_____

Today I am confessing...

_____

_____

Today I am praying for...

_____

_____

My reflections...

_____

_____

Day Six

What might it look like to be double minded?

Today I praise God for...

Today I am confessing...

Today I am praying for...

My reflections...

Day Seven

How can a doubt-filled prayer life cause chaos and disorder in your life?

_____

_____

_____

Today I praise God for...

_____

_____

Today I am confessing...

_____

_____

Today I am praying for...

_____

_____

My reflections...

_____

_____

Answer me when I call, God, who vindicates me. You freed me from affliction; be gracious to me and hear my prayer.

Psalm 4:1

Week 10

Praying in the Spirit

In the same way the Spirit also joins to help in our weakness, because we do not know what to pray for as we should, but the Spirit Himself intercedes for us with unspoken groanings. And He who searches the hearts knows the Spirit's mind-set, because He intercedes for the saints according to the will of God.
Romans 8:26-27

Praying was always a mystery to me. I never quite figured it out, and it was hard to get into a habit. I especially didn't like public prayer—I felt silly praying out loud, and I didn't like all the pressure. In my faith tradition, prayers were never scripted, unlike sermons, so it was a burden to get up to the front and lead the group in an unscripted prayer.

Prayer was hard until I took a class in college called "Counseling for Ministers." It was a semester of tips on how to counsel churchgoers in their times of need. What I learned about prayer in that class stuck out to me the most—I never considered prayer as part of a counseling

session! Since spoken prayer is so important in counseling, the teacher urged us to pray before we prayed. The advice was to "pray in the Spirit." As we bowed our heads, we were told to take a few moments of silence to ask the Spirit to guide our words. Then, we'd launch into speaking the prayer aloud. Something remarkable happened when I did this. The Spirit clearly worked in the prayer!

This isn't just a trick for pastors though. Everyone can access the power of the Spirit in prayer. When we don't have the words to say, the Spirit intercedes on our behalf. What does the Spirit interceding look like? It might be that you are pointed to a particular passage of Scripture or might feel the sudden urge to stop and pray for someone or something. Maybe the Spirit gives you the strength to talk to God when you don't feel like praying at all.

In the context of Romans 8, Paul is writing of the troubling times in the world. He says we can't see the future, but we can have faith and hope. Later in the chapter, Paul passionately preaches that as Spirit-filled believers, we will triumph. We don't always know what to pray for because we are imperfect and don't know what our earthly future holds. But that's why we have the Spirit interceding for us! Consider starting your prayers by praying in the Spirit, invite the Holy Spirit to take over and guide you when communicating with God.

Heavenly Father, we thank You for the gift of the Spirit in our lives. Spirit, come and intercede for me. Guide my heart as I lift it toward God. Help me to rely on You as I try to live a life that glorifies God with every breath. Amen.

Written by Jake Doberenz

Day One

How can I listen for the Spirit's work in my prayer life?

Today I praise God for...

Today I am confessing...

Today I am praying for...

My reflections...

Day Two

How can praying out loud help those around me?

Today I praise God for...

Today I am confessing...

Today I am praying for...

My reflections...

Day Three

Why is prayer so important that the Spirit must get involved?

Today I praise God for...

Today I am confessing...

Today I am praying for...

My reflections...

120

Day Four

What topics do I tend to avoid when I pray to God?

_____
_____
_____

Today I praise God for...

_____
_____

Today I am confessing...

_____
_____

Today I am praying for...

_____
_____

My reflections...

_____
_____

Day Five

Why might we ignore the role of the Spirit in our prayer life?

Today I praise God for...

Today I am confessing...

Today I am praying for...

My reflections...

Day Six

How can Spirit-guided prayer help me grow in my faith in God?

Today I praise God for...

Today I am confessing...

Today I am praying for...

My reflections...

Day Seven

How can I make praying in the Spirit my routine?

_____

_____

_____

Today I praise God for...

_____

_____

Today I am confessing...

_____

_____

Today I am praying for...

_____

_____

My reflections...

_____

_____

Write for us and have your
devotion featured online at
devotableapp.com/contribute

Is anyone among you suffering? He should pray. Is anyone cheerful? He should sing praises.
James 5:13

Week 11

Call Upon Me

You will call to Me and come and pray to Me, and I will listen to you. You will seek Me and find Me when you search for Me with all your heart.
Jeremiah 29:12-13

Some time ago, I was reading through the comments section of a blog I follow. The person commenting noted that whenever someone told her of an issue they were facing or an issue in general, she would tell them she would pray for them. But then, something changed, and she started either offering to pray for them right then if she thought they were receptive, or she would quietly do it, still in the moment, if she wasn't sure. It didn't need to be a long, elaborate prayer.

I'm learning that God doesn't need long, elaborate, or flowery prayers. He just needs a sincere heart. I've recently adopted that praying in the moment philosophy. For a very long time, if someone suggested/ requested I pray for something, and I tried to wait until bedtime, when I usually said my prayers, my tendency was to forget. I am human, and I have a gazillion other things on my mind. So now when someone asks me to pray, I make sure to do it right away. Or, if I hear of a need in

conversation, and there is an opportunity to pray with the person, I do. It not only offers comfort to the person I'm praying with, but it humbles me.

I once had an Instagram follow request from someone I didn't know. The young lady had Jeremiah 29:11 in her intro. I looked it up, and kept reading through verse 14. Wow! God himself tells me that when I pray He listens to me. He has certain requirements though; He wants us to seek Him with all our hearts. I don't know about you, but I've struggled with giving God all my heart. Sometimes I think if I can just fix it up a little, or I can stop doing some of the things I'm doing, then I can give Him all of me. But I don't think He wants me to wait for that. He wants all of me, just the way I am, at this very moment. And He promises to hear my prayers when I seek Him.

Dear Heavenly Father, we come seeking You. Remind us that we do not need to be perfect to come to You, we just need to come, and You will make us perfect through You and Your love. Help us remember to come to You first and boldly, because You promised to hear us.

Written by Kaysian Gordon

Day One

How can you adopt an attitude of praying right away so you don't forget?

Today I praise God for...

Today I am confessing...

Today I am praying for...

My reflections...

Day Two

What are some things holding you back from completely committing
to God?

Today I praise God for...

Today I am confessing...

Today I am praying for...

My reflections...

Day Three

Did you realize that Jeremiah 29:11 was a contingent promise?

_____

_____

_____

Today I praise God for...

_____

_____

Today I am confessing...

_____

_____

Today I am praying for...

_____

_____

My reflections...

_____

_____

Day Four

What is the difference between an outright promise and a contingent promise found in the Bible?

Today I praise God for...

Today I am confessing...

Today I am praying for...

My reflections...

Day Five

Have you ever had the urge to "randomly" pray for someone? What did you do?

Today I praise God for...

Today I am confessing...

Today I am praying for...

My reflections...

Day Six

Are you concerned that you or your prayers are not "good enough"?

Today I praise God for...

Today I am confessing...

Today I am praying for...

My reflections...

Day Seven

How do you combat the lie of fearing that you are not good enough to approach God's throne in prayer?

_____

_____

_____

Today I praise God for...

_____

_____

Today I am confessing...

_____

_____

Today I am praying for...

_____

_____

My reflections...

_____

_____

Now this is the confidence we have before Him: Whenever we ask anything according to His will, He hears us.

1 John 5:14

Week 12

Praying the Beatitudes

The poor in spirit are blessed, for the kingdom of heaven is theirs. Those who mourn are blessed, for they will be comforted.
Matthew 5:3-4

Have you ever reached into a bag of your favorite chips anticipating flavor heaven, only to bite into the equivalent of salty cardboard? At times, my prayer life gets stale and flavorless too. And it's just as

disappointing. I sit down with my journal and write down what comes to mind. But my mind can be a pretty shallow pool from which to draw. My needs and concerns, even my thanks and praise, can get pretty rote. The same things come up over and over again, and left to my own devices, what should be a two-way conversation can get pretty one-sided. Not to mention selfish. That's why I've started praying a lot of Scripture.

"All scripture is inspired by God [literally breathed out by God] and is profitable for teaching, for rebuking, for correcting, for training in righteousness." (2 Timothy 3:16) Since the Bible's words are the Words

of God (by way of the Holy Spirit - 2 Peter 1:21), and this verse tells us that ALL of it is profitable, when I pray Scripture I know I am praying perfectly within God's will.

Sometimes I search the Bible for a Scripture on a certain topic or situation. But more often than not, as I study, I just feel drawn to pray specific verses or passages over my family. Lately I'm fascinated with the idea of praying the Beatitudes.

The word beatitude means blessing. There are many places in the Bible, especially in Psalms, where blessings are promised or bestowed. But the only spot where more than two or three blessings are listed together is the recording of Jesus' Sermon on the Mount in Matthew. All of these blessings refer to the future kingdom of heaven. Not to be mistaken with things we would consider blessings in the here and now. God owes us nothing, of course. But because of the work of Jesus, He promises us everything in due time.

When reading the Beatitudes, it's important to understand that Jesus was not referencing a certain group or type of people. These promises are for anyone who allows the presence of God to manifest in his/her life. If God wants to bless those who possess these characteristics, then I want them! My sin nature gets in the way, though. I need His divine help to be merciful and meek and pure in heart. So I'm asking for these things in prayer.

Lord, I've spent far too long selfishly praying for You to bless me. Today I ask that You make me into someone You can bless. In my flesh, I am the polar opposite of the person Jesus preached about. But I'm asking You to take possession of my heart and mind so my thoughts and actions look more like You.

Written by Lauren Sparks

Day One

In what areas do you rely too much on yourself and not the omnipotence of God?

_____

_____

_____

Today I praise God for...

_____

_____

Today I am confessing...

_____

_____

Today I am praying for...

_____

_____

My reflections...

_____

_____

Day Two

Spend some time confessing your sins and praying against the evil in the world. Do you have specific sins you need to confess today?

Today I praise God for...

Today I am confessing...

Today I am praying for...

My reflections...

Day Three

Ask God to show you relationships that need an extra dose of supernatural meekness, gentleness, and self-control.
What relationships are those?

Today I praise God for...

Today I am confessing...

Today I am praying for...

My reflections...

Day Four

In what areas of your life are you struggling with obedience?

_____

_____

_____

Today I praise God for...

_____

Today I am confessing...

_____

Today I am praying for...

_____

My reflections...

_____

Day Five

Is there someone you need to forgive or someone who needs a hand up?

_____

_____

_____

Today I praise God for...

_____

_____

Today I am confessing...

_____

_____

Today I am praying for...

_____

_____

My reflections...

_____

_____

Day Six

Are there movies, TV shows, music, or websites you would steer clear of if you could see Jesus sitting beside you?

Today I praise God for...

Today I am confessing...

Today I am praying for...

My reflections...

Day Seven

Where do you see a lack of peace in the world around you?

_____

_____

_____

Today I praise God for...

_____

_____

Today I am confessing...

_____

_____

Today I am praying for...

_____

_____

My reflections...

_____

_____

Subscribe to our email list for
more daily devotions at
devotableapp.com/subscribe

First of all, then, I urge that petitions, prayers, intercessions, and thanksgivings be made for everyone.

1 Timothy 2:1

Week 13

Turning Our Worry Into Prayer

Don't worry about anything, but in everything, through prayer and petition with thanksgiving, let your requests be made known to God. And the peace of God, which surpasses every thought, will guard your hearts and minds in Christ Jesus.
Philippians 4:6-7

If there is one command in Scripture I repeatedly fail to obey it is, "Don't worry." As someone who comes from a long line of worriers and possesses a vivid imagination, it is all too easy for me to imagine any number of potential disaster scenarios, and it is definitely not the path to peace!

I've lost count of the number of times people have quoted these verses from Philippians, telling me to pray. The problem is: even when I pray, I still worry!

A few years ago, facing a situation that was fraught with worry, I realised I finally had to find a way to put these verses into action - to hand my worries to God and leave them there.

I came up with the idea of a worry box.

I wrote all the things I worried about on small slips of paper. There were over thirty of them at first! Once I finished, I began to pray about them, taking each slip of paper, bringing the worry to God, then folding it up, and placing it in the box. I decided I would review the worries in a week's time; until then I was going to try not to think about them. This was no easy task, but looking at the box was a tangible reminder that I had given the worries to God.

In the meantime, I looked up some Bible verses that reassured me. I tried to find the promises of God that spoke into the worries: reminders of God's power, His love, His plan to work all things together for good, and that He was with me. I wrote out a selection of these verses and aimed to read them each day, thanking God for His promises.

After a week, it was time to open the worry box. I removed each slip and read it. Some worries had been resolved, so I was able to dispose of those, thanking God for His help. Other worries remained, so I prayed about those and returned them to the box. There were also new worries to add. Then I left them for another week. It was a simple yet effective practice. While it didn't cure my worry habit entirely, it did get me through that anxious season by helping me give my worries to God, and as I did so, I gradually began to experience more of His peace.

Lord, thank You that we can bring our worries to You, knowing You care and have the power to help us. Please help us learn to hand our worries to You, hold to Your promises, and experience Your peace. Amen.

Written by Lesley Crawford

Day One

What things are worrying you today?

Today I praise God for...

Today I am confessing...

Today I am praying for...

My reflections...

Day Two

How do your worries affect your life and disrupt your peace?

Today I praise God for...

Today I am confessing...

Today I am praying for...

My reflections...

Day Three

How can prayer help in dealing with your worries?

_____

_____

_____

Today I praise God for...

_____

_____

Today I am confessing...

_____

_____

Today I am praying for...

_____

_____

My reflections...

_____

_____

Day Four

What truths about God's character could reassure you when you are worried?

Today I praise God for...

Today I am confessing...

Today I am praying for...

My reflections...

Day Five

What promises of God could you focus on to help you with your worries?

_____

_____

_____

Today I praise God for...

_____

_____

Today I am confessing...

_____

_____

Today I am praying for...

_____

_____

My reflections...

_____

_____

Day Six

How has God helped you with your worries in the past?

_____

_____

_____

Today I praise God for...

_____

_____

Today I am confessing...

_____

_____

Today I am praying for...

_____

_____

My reflections...

_____

_____

Day Seven

What practical steps could you take to work towards handing your worries over to God and focusing on his promises?

Today I praise God for...

Today I am confessing...

Today I am praying for...

My reflections...

About midnight Paul and Silas were praying and singing hymns to God, and the prisoners were listening to them.

Acts 16:25

Week 14

When We Don't Know

I pray that the perception of your mind may be enlightened so you may know what is the hope of His calling, what are the glorious riches of His inheritance among the saints, and what is the immeasurable greatness of His power to us who believe, according to the working of His vast strength. Ephesians 1:18-19

We often seek advice from people who have "been there"—those who have experience in a struggle we're facing. We seek consolation from people who have experienced what we're about to face. The Apostle Paul's outlook and focus on prayer are from the perspective of one who had suffered and remained faithful.

Paul, through the power of the Holy Spirit, wrote several New Testament books. In his letters, we read instruction, correction, and encouragement. But what speaks most loudly, are his prayers for God's people. The man who gave his life to spread the Gospel suffered hardships, shipwrecks, betrayal, and imprisonment, yet his prayers focused on spiritual well-being. He gives us lessons from experience

about how to pray for eternal purposes.

When we don't know what to pray, Paul's prayers guide us to focus on a process and character development, not a requested response. One of Paul's most profound prayers is found in Ephesians 3:14-20. He begins his prayer with, "For this reason." He gives us the basis for his prayer in the preceding verses: we have "every spiritual blessing in Christ." (1:3) God delights in pouring out His blessings from His glorious riches. What are those blessings and riches? Paul's prayer tells us: being strengthened with power in our inner being, for Christ to dwell in our hearts, to be rooted and established in love, to grasp the infinite love of God, and being filled with the fullness of God.

No, we don't see a request for healing but for strength. Not an answer to a decision, but knowing Christ in us will direct our steps; no resolution to a conflict, but through the Spirit I can live in the love of God and share that with others. When we don't know how or what to pray look at Paul's model: strength, love, direction, and the fullness of God. The process is more important than the answer. Paul closes with one final confident reminder, "Now to Him who is able to do above and beyond all that we ask or think according to the power that works in us." (Ephesians 3:20) Yes, God's desired outcome surpasses mine.

Father, thank You for the examples from the apostle Paul of praying for godly character. Help me not to desire a quick fix or easy way out, but to pray for spiritual growth for myself and others. Amen.

Written by Marilyn Nutter

Day One

Read Ephesians 3:14-20. What are the prayer requests Paul makes?

_____

_____

Today I praise God for...

_____

Today I am confessing...

_____

Today I am praying for...

_____

My reflections...

_____

Day Two

Is Paul's list different from the prayer requests you usually make?
Does this motivate you to change the way you pray?

_____

_____

_____

Today I praise God for...

_____

_____

Today I am confessing...

_____

_____

Today I am praying for...

_____

_____

My reflections...

_____

_____

Day Three

How do Paul's prayers bring you into a deeper relationship with Christ?

Today I praise God for...

Today I am confessing...

Today I am praying for...

My reflections...

Day Four

How does godly character develop if we pray using Paul's model instead of praying to "fix" a problem or resolve a difficulty?

Today I praise God for...

Today I am confessing...

Today I am praying for...

My reflections...

Day Five

Make a list of people you pray for on a regular basis. Insert their names in the verses in Ephesians 3:16-19.

_____

_____

_____

Today I praise God for...

_____

_____

Today I am confessing...

_____

_____

Today I am praying for...

_____

_____

My reflections...

_____

_____

Day Six

What does it mean that God can do "above and beyond" what I ask?
Do we limit God by asking for something specific?

Today I praise God for...

Today I am confessing...

Today I am praying for...

My reflections...

Day Seven

Look up the other prayers Paul wrote. Insert your name in them.

_____

_____

_____

Today I praise God for...

_____

_____

Today I am confessing...

_____

_____

Today I am praying for...

_____

_____

My reflections...

_____

_____

Listen to all of our devotions on
our podcast at
devotableapp.com/podcast

When He reached the place, He told them, "Pray that you may not enter into temptation."
Luke 22:40

Week 15

Learning to Listen

[Eli] told Samuel, 'Go and lie down. If He calls you, say, "Speak, Lord, for Your servant is listening."' So Samuel went and lay down in his place. The Lord came, stood there, and called as before, 'Samuel, Samuel!' Samuel responded, 'Speak, for Your servant is listening.'
1 Samuel 3:9-10

I am a talker. Many people who are close to me can attest to this. I like to have good conversations. The only problem is that at times I dominate the conversation, and it can become one-sided. The same problem can infect my prayer life. All too often my prayers become a monologue, and no longer even resemble a conversation between God and me. It's just me talking and begging God to listen, but never offering to do the same. This story from 1 Samuel 3 reminds me of two valuable truths about prayer.

First, the truth that prayer is, at its simplest definition, a conversation between us and God. Although too often we cannot seem to differentiate the voice of God from the voice of the world. In

the Gospel of John, Jesus says this of his followers, "My sheep hear My voice, I know them, and they follow Me." (John 10:27) The sheep could discern the voice of the Shepherd. They could trust what they were hearing, because they knew they could trust the voice that was speaking. We must know the voice of the Shepherd to be able to trust what we're hearing, and the best way to do that is to familiarize ourselves with who Jesus is, and how God has spoken in the past. This requires us to start with one basic step - learn more about the Shepherd. Read about who God is, how God interacts. We need to learn more about His personality and characteristics, and the best way to do this is to read your Bible.

Second, to listen effectively we must be quiet. There is so much noise in our world today. Everyone is talking, and no one is listening. Whether on the news, in the classroom, at Thanksgiving dinner with your relatives; people are talking but absolutely no one is listening. Many times, I wonder, "Why isn't God speaking to me?" and the more fitting question, "Why am I not listening?" I am so busy talking, laying out every concern, request, praise, and frustration, that I never stop to listen for God's response. To hear the voice of God, we must be willing to stop talking and actually listen for the whisper of God. We must learn to hear and discern the voice of God, so when we're in the position of Samuel we can respond likewise, "Speak, for your servant is listening."

Father God, help us to learn how to listen. Help us to embrace the same posture as Samuel and be willing to quiet ourselves and discern Your voice out from amongst the world. Speak, Lord, I'm listening. Amen.

Written by Matthew Spear

Day One

When you pray, do you tend to talk more than listen? Why?

Today I praise God for...

Today I am confessing...

Today I am praying for...

My reflections...

Day Two

Have you ever thought "Why doesn't God speak as often now?" How has that impacted your prayer life?

_____

_____

_____

Today I praise God for...

_____

_____

Today I am confessing...

_____

_____

Today I am praying for...

_____

_____

My reflections...

_____

_____

Day Three

Have you ever heard the voice of God, either audibly, in a dream, or while you're reading the Bible? What did you hear?

Today I praise God for...

Today I am confessing...

Today I am praying for...

My reflections...

Day Four

What are some steps you could take this week to begin to know the Shepherd better?

Today I praise God for...

Today I am confessing...

Today I am praying for...

My reflections...

Day Five

Think about how you usually pray; time of day, place, posture. Then, try setting aside 10 minutes just to listen.

Today I praise God for...

Today I am confessing...

Today I am praying for...

My reflections...

Day Six

Think about the passage from 1 Samuel. Why is it so hard for us to respond to God with "Speak, Lord, your servant is listening"?

Today I praise God for...

Today I am confessing...

Today I am praying for...

My reflections...

Day Seven

Why is it so hard for us to discern the voice of God in our lives?

_____

_____

_____

Today I praise God for...

_____

_____

Today I am confessing...

_____

_____

Today I am praying for...

_____

_____

My reflections...

_____

_____

And My people who are called by My name humble themselves, pray and seek My face, and turn from their evil ways, then I will hear from heaven, forgive their sin, and heal their land.

2 Chronicles 7:14

Week 16

Facing Your Giants in Prayer

On the day I called, you answered me; You increased strength within me.
Psalm 138:3

Each day we are faced with seemingly hopeless situations. Ones that are entirely out of our control. With that lack of control comes a weakness that brings us to our knees. It is in that intimate time with God that we can lay both our weakness and powerlessness down at His feet. By allowing God to enter our most difficult circumstances, "our giants", through prayer, we give up our weakness and allow Him to shine through with His mighty strength and power.

God is bigger than any problem we may face. Our prayers, even in moments of hopelessness and despair, are heard by an awesome God.

Throughout Scripture we repeatedly hear about God's character that is filled with power, authority, strength, and hope! Over and over, God is referred to as a lion. Lions are considered the kings of the jungle with characteristics such as strength, fearlessness, power, boldness, and beauty. Their roars are said to be heard from miles away, scaring

off predators, communicating their fierceness, and establishing their territory.

Scripture talks about God's roar and His power over our lives. In Hosea 11:10 we read, "They will follow the LORD; he will roar like a lion. When he roars, his children will come trembling from the west." God's roar is not one we should fear, but instead one we should embrace. When God speaks, He speaks from a posture of love and protection. By understanding His character and His control over the situations in our lives, we can know with full confidence that God is working behind the scenes to bring good from all things.

By taking "our giants", our most difficult circumstances directly to God in prayer, He unleashes His power and authority over every situation. David poured out his heart to God in prayer remembering God's goodness, finding hope and comfort from his afflictions. Despite "giants" in David's life, he simply prayed, and God answered. David trusted in God's character and authority over the circumstances he faced. God took his weakness and replaced it with abundant strength, strength that conquered his "giants." God wants to do the same in our lives. Our God is a God of restoration and hope, strength, and power. Have you taken time today to sit at His feet, praying for His strength in facing your "giants"?

Dear Heavenly Father, Thank You for Your strength and power in our lives. Help us to remember that nothing we face is too big for You to handle. In Jesus' name, Amen.

Written by Pamela Keener

Day One

Do you have any circumstances that you feel are out of your control, ones that have left you weak and without hope? Write down what things have stolen your peace and lay them at God's feet.

Today I praise God for...

Today I am confessing...

Today I am praying for...

My reflections...

Day Two

Prayerfully reflect on God's character. List five things that reflect
who God is to you and how you see Him.

Today I praise God for...

Today I am confessing...

Today I am praying for...

My reflections...

Day Three

Write down three things that have happened in your life that remind you of the previously mentioned characteristics of God.

Today I praise God for...

Today I am confessing...

Today I am praying for...

My reflections...

Day Four

Looking back at your "giants", which one is robbing you the most of your peace?

Today I praise God for...

Today I am confessing...

Today I am praying for...

My reflections...

Day Five

Think about how you would like to see God move in your life with respect to this "giant"?

_____

_____

_____

Today I praise God for...

_____

_____

Today I am confessing...

_____

_____

Today I am praying for...

_____

_____

My reflections...

_____

_____

Day Six

Write out a prayer asking God for help in trusting Him fully with your "giant" instead of trying to control it yourself.

Today I praise God for...

Today I am confessing...

Today I am praying for...

My reflections...

Day Seven

Write out a heartfelt prayer and spend some time talking with God about your "giants."

Today I praise God for...

Today I am confessing...

Today I am praying for...

My reflections...

Read and discover more free
devotions at
devotableapp.com

When they had prayed, the place where they were assembled was shaken, and they were all filled with the Holy Spirit and began to speak God's message with boldness.

Acts 4:31

Week 17

Focused On Distractions:
What's Holding Your Prayer Back

Devote yourselves to prayer; stay alert in it with thanksgiving.
Colossians 4:2

We present all sorts of prayers that can range from diligent to desperate, devoted to delirious. It often hinges on why we're approaching the throne of the Lord at that moment. We should not approach prayer the same way we approach singing the ABCs. When's the last time you sounded out the phonetic sound of each letter as if you were teaching a child? Typically, we fire off those twenty-six letters without a second thought about what unique contribution each individual letter provides to written English. Thus, there is no longer a total alertness to the power. Sure, we know what they can do, but do we appreciate what can be done with them? Knowing and actually appreciating are totally different. Remaining alert in prayer requires minimizing or eliminating distractions for one.

The devil will try to drive you crazy to the point that you're so delirious your prayer becomes weak and powerless. He strives to tire

you out emotionally, spiritually, physically, and financially. The next thing you know you're just trying to get done with your prayer instead of being in the moment and savoring the opportunity and experience of being with Jesus Christ our Lord and Savior.

You know, most cities or states have a local law against texting and driving because it distracts us and is a tremendous safety risk. Yet, in a world fighting for our attention, we allow things to distract us from praying and that's as dangerous as it gets. When we rush through prayers to maximize time online or getting to an appointment in the morning, we sacrifice focus, not really thinking about the consequences of sending up a half-hearted prayer to the Lord and expecting a miracle in return. Yet, we'll complain that God isn't paying us the attention we feel is warranted. The irony of wondering if He is alert and alive while we deliriously deliver dead prayers.

Paul dropped a jewel for the rest of us to pick up. He said that even though you are going to keep praying, you can't get numb to it. Be so into it, so alert that your thanksgiving continually anchors you.

Wonderful Counselor, I choose to present a fully aware prayer. Let these words of thanksgiving be pure and undiluted by thoughts or actions joined with outside forces. As I call on Your mighty name, consecrate this renewed petition in my heart. Amen.

Written by Quentin G. Love

Day One

Do you get distracted while praying? Why?

_____

_____

_____

Today I praise God for...

_____

_____

Today I am confessing...

_____

_____

Today I am praying for...

_____

_____

My reflections...

_____

_____

Day Two

How can you avoid having routine prayers while making sure you don't wander unnecessarily?

_____

_____

_____

Today I praise God for...

_____

_____

Today I am confessing...

_____

_____

Today I am praying for...

_____

_____

My reflections...

_____

_____

Day Three

What are three ways you can work to keep your prayers focused and not delirious?

Today I praise God for...

Today I am confessing...

Today I am praying for...

My reflections...

Day Four

Is there anything you're more devoted to than prayer?

_____

_____

_____

Today I praise God for...

_____

_____

Today I am confessing...

_____

_____

Today I am praying for...

_____

_____

My reflections...

_____

_____

Day Five

Can you list five habits that would be helpful for keeping your prayer on track?

Today I praise God for...

Today I am confessing...

Today I am praying for...

My reflections...

Day Six

Do you keep a prayer list?

Today I praise God for...

Today I am confessing...

Today I am praying for...

My reflections...

Day Seven

Are there any new Scriptures about prayer you can find this week?

Today I praise God for...

Today I am confessing...

Today I am praying for...

My reflections...

For I know the plans I have for you"—this is the Lord's declaration—"plans for your welfare, not for disaster, to give you a future and a hope.
Jeremiah 29:11

Week 18

Why Small Prayers Matter

'Because of your little faith,' He told them. 'For I assure you: If you have faith the size of a mustard seed, you will tell this mountain, "Move from here to there," and it will move. Nothing will be impossible for you.'
Matthew 17:20

Do small prayers seem silly to you? Maybe you feel okay approaching God with the big things, like health scares, accidents, job losses, or marriage crises. But what about the everyday small things? Do they really matter to God?

The truth is, the smallest things in our lives greatly matter to God. He has numbered all the hairs on our heads (Matthew 10:30). Jesus used parables about small things like flowers, birds, grains of salt, and yeast to teach us spiritual truths. God notices the small things and deeply cares about all the details in your life. Your small prayers really do count in His eyes.

For example, the slow driver in front of you may be a small matter in your day. But this situation probably causes you frustration and possibly anger. If you lift that small matter up to God, He will grant you perspective, patience, and peace in the moment. God will comfort

you as you bring small prayers to Him.

Another example is dealing with a difficult person. Perhaps this person isn't harming or insulting you; they are just getting on your nerves. In the moment of irritation, you can offer up your feelings in prayer. God will help you be kind, compassionate, and loving through His power. He will use small prayers to make you more like Jesus.

Our small prayers help us cultivate a more trusting relationship with God. Instead of approaching Him only when big things happen, you can meet God every day with smaller prayers. Invite Him into your smaller matters, and your faith will grow. Ask Him to help you study for a test, prepare a report, or teach your child a new skill. By covering these smaller matters in prayer, you will see God at work in your life. He will give you more joy, peace, and hope as you carry small matters up to Him in prayer.

If your faith is as small as a mustard seed, it can still move mountains. Our small prayers can also do wonderful things for God's glory. They can be even more effective than one big prayer, because He will use them as seeds to grow your faith. Be faithful in offering small prayers to God. The more seeds you plant, the more fruitful your faith will be. Try offering small prayers every day this week and watch your trust in God expand.

Lord, I trust You with all my prayers, even ones about small matters. Everything that happens in my life matters to You. I want my faith to grow as I speak small prayers. Help me see more of You in the smallest things, so my trust in You can expand. Amen.

Written by Sarah Geringer

Day One

How can small prayers help you in your faith journey right now?

_____

_____

_____

Today I praise God for...

_____

_____

Today I am confessing...

_____

_____

Today I am praying for...

_____

_____

My reflections...

_____

_____

Day Two

Which relationship of yours could benefit from small prayers?

_____

_____

_____

Today I praise God for...

_____

Today I am confessing...

_____

Today I am praying for...

_____

My reflections...

_____

Day Three

Which situation at home, school, or work needs your small prayers?

_____

_____

_____

Today I praise God for...

_____

_____

Today I am confessing...

_____

_____

Today I am praying for...

_____

_____

My reflections...

_____

_____

Day Four

What time of day is best for you to offer small prayers?

Today I praise God for...

Today I am confessing...

Today I am praying for...

My reflections...

Day Five

Can you name three situations that you can turn into small prayers?

_____

_____

_____

Today I praise God for...

_____

_____

Today I am confessing...

_____

_____

Today I am praying for...

_____

_____

My reflections...

_____

_____

Day Six

Which area do you think God wants you to cover in small, consistent prayers?

Today I praise God for...

Today I am confessing...

Today I am praying for...

My reflections...

Day Seven

How can small prayers reinforce the fact that nothing is impossible with God?

_____

_____

_____

Today I praise God for...

_____

_____

Today I am confessing...

_____

_____

Today I am praying for...

_____

_____

My reflections...

_____

_____

Support us or partner with us
as we try to reach more people
with the Gospel at
devotableapp.com/contribute

Stay awake and pray, so that you won't enter into temptation. The spirit is willing, but the flesh is weak.

Matthew 26:41

Week 19

Depend on God's Favor

For His anger lasts only a moment, but His favor, a lifetime. Weeping may spend the night, but there is joy in the morning.
Psalm 30:5

I used to not understand why I didn't get the answers even after I prayed so hard for someone or something. Why didn't I see any changes?

I had fully trusted in God. I even believed I could move "that mountain." So... why am I still struggling and so desperate for help? Why does He seem to be doing nothing?

Later on, I came to realize that He loves me more than anyone else does. He loves that person that I'm praying for more than anyone else, including me. And yes, He loves YOU more than anyone else in this world does. Doesn't God only design the best things for those He loves? He knows our hearts. He understands our situations, and He sees you and me. When you don't understand what is going on, trust His heart and His love for you. He only intends to give us the best.

Genesis 50:20 states, "You planned evil against me; God planned it for good to bring about the present result—the survival of many people."

Whatever you are facing right now will more than likely only last for a season, but His favor in your life will last a lifetime. God wants to see us walk by faith all the time and keep our faith in Him during the hard seasons. He wants us to learn how to fully trust in Him alone.

Prayer is the breath of every Christian. So, keep praying. Pray with all your heart, and with all your might. As it says in Psalm 30:5b, "Weeping may spend the night, but there is joy in the morning." Pray without ceasing, cry out to God, keep reminding Him, and don't get discouraged though you haven't seen any answers yet. When the morning comes, lift up your head and walk victoriously, as if you have won the battle and as if you have seen the answers. Keep praying and leave it to Him. Depend on Him and on His favor, and you will not be disappointed. You are safe in His arms, for He is not only a loving God, but also a mighty God.

Thank You for keeping me from falling apart. Forgive my doubts, my disbelief, and my selfishness. Teach me how to pray earnestly and help me to see You clearer in every situation. Open my heart to understand there's a purpose in everything that happens, and You intend it for my good. Teach me to bless Your name at all times, for You deserve all glory. I thank You for yesterday, today, and tomorrow. In Jesus' name, Amen.

Written by Stephanie Caesara

Day One

Is there anything in your life you have prayed for and not received? Why might that be?

_____

_____

_____

Today I praise God for...

_____

_____

Today I am confessing...

_____

_____

Today I am praying for...

_____

_____

My reflections...

_____

_____

Day Two

Have you thought about why God loves you despite any of the situations you're facing right now?

Today I praise God for...

Today I am confessing...

Today I am praying for...

My reflections...

Day Three

Have you prayed continually?

Today I praise God for...

Today I am confessing...

Today I am praying for...

My reflections...

Day Four

If He doesn't answer you, or if the answer is "no", will you still trust in Him?

_____

_____

Today I praise God for...

_____

Today I am confessing...

_____

Today I am praying for...

_____

My reflections...

_____

Day Five

Why is prayer so important?

_____

_____

_____

Today I praise God for...

_____

_____

Today I am confessing...

_____

_____

Today I am praying for...

_____

_____

My reflections...

_____

_____

Day Six

A prayerless Christian is an impotent Christian, so have you been a prayerful Christian?

Today I praise God for...

Today I am confessing...

Today I am praying for...

My reflections...

Day Seven

How has prayer changed you?

_____

_____

_____

Today I praise God for...

_____

_____

Today I am confessing...

_____

_____

Today I am praying for...

_____

_____

My reflections...

_____

_____

He then told them a parable on the need for them to pray always and not become discouraged.
Luke 18:1

Week 20

Prayer - Key to the First Church's Power and Unity

All these were continually united in prayer.
Acts 1:14a

Power is often misunderstood and misused. When directed for a good purpose it can be beneficial. But when misused it's destructive and disruptive. If coerced, a unity based in fear and deception can be wielded into a powerful force for evil. Religious leaders stirred up a crowd of people who became a mob with a unified cry of, "Crucify Him!" But God worked His purposes for our reconciliation by grace with the all-powerful God whose nature is love.

In those early days of fear and uncertainty, how did a small group of believers become a unified community filled with God's power? Prayer! Prayer was the key to the power and unity of the first church. It still is for any church and it begins with each of us. Logic says we need to get people to believe and do the same things. But this results in conformity and uniformity. Not unity. Coercion through compulsion is not godly power.

But let's be honest, prayer seems like a non-action. It's more like

surrender than overcoming. Exactly! Prayer is an action word and it begins with our surrender to the Lord and His will. Jesus is our prime example— from His times of solitude in prayer seen throughout the gospels to His anguished prayer in Gethsemane. Surrendering is an act of our free will. Jesus doesn't coerce us to do so, and the Holy Spirit isn't hovering over us like a helicopter parent to remind us to pray.

When Jesus told His followers to wait in Jerusalem for the promise of the Father (Acts1:4), He didn't give more details than that. They didn't know what to expect, but they knew to prayerfully wait. They prayed—continually with one purpose!

What happened after their ten days of continuing in prayer as a group? The Lord sent His Spirit upon them as they waited with one accord in one place (Acts 2:1). Prayer was the foundation of their unity and God's power at work in and through them. When the new church faced a great challenge, they raised their voices to God with one accord. The place where they were assembled was shaken, and they were filled with the Holy Spirit.

If you want unity and power in your church, then choose to pray. Commit to consistent, regular prayer, on your own and together with other believers. Don't wait for others to take the lead or join you. Choose to surrender and learn to wait on God in prayer as the early church did—even when you don't know what to expect. This is the key to power and unity in the church—unified prayer!

Lord help me to commit to consistent prayer, to learn how to wait on You as I surrender myself and trust that You will fill me and unify Your church with Your power.

Written by Trip Kimball

Day One

When is the best time of the day for you to pray and intercede for others?

Today I praise God for...

Today I am confessing...

Today I am praying for...

My reflections...

Day Two

How consistent are you in prayer on your own and with other believers?

_____

_____

_____

Today I praise God for...

_____

_____

Today I am confessing...

_____

_____

Today I am praying for...

_____

_____

My reflections...

_____

_____

Day Three

How often do you pray for your church fellowship and others?

_____

_____

_____

Today I praise God for...

_____

_____

Today I am confessing...

_____

_____

Today I am praying for...

_____

_____

My reflections...

_____

_____

Day Four

What makes it difficult for you to surrender your will to the Lord?

_____

_____

_____

Today I praise God for...

_____

_____

Today I am confessing...

_____

_____

Today I am praying for...

_____

_____

My reflections...

_____

_____

Day Five

How has the Lord honored the time you spend waiting on Him in prayer?

_____

_____

_____

Today I praise God for...

_____

_____

Today I am confessing...

_____

_____

Today I am praying for...

_____

_____

My reflections...

_____

_____

Day Six

What are specific answers you've seen to your prayers for your church?

Today I praise God for...

Today I am confessing...

Today I am praying for...

My reflections...

Day Seven

How have you encouraged others by praying for them and with them?

Today I praise God for...

Today I am confessing...

Today I am praying for...

My reflections...

Write for us and have your
devotion featured online at
devotableapp.com/contribute

The sacrifice of the wicked is detestable to the Lord, but the prayer of the upright is His delight.

Proverbs 15:8

Week 21

Remember Who You're Talking To

Therefore you should pray like this: Our Father in Heaven, Your name be honored as holy.
Matthew 6:9

"Remember who you're talking to!" Most of us have probably been on the receiving end of this familiar rebuke at one time or another growing up. Learning how to show appropriate respect to our superiors is an important, though not always pleasant, life lesson. But it is one we can observe quite clearly in Matthew 6:9 as Jesus lays out a framework for how we should pray. From the very first sentence, Jesus sets the tone for the remainder of the prayer. He directs our attention toward God's holiness and invites us to enter into His presence with an attitude of reverence and worship.

Sadly, it is a necessary reminder for modern day Christians, functioning in a culture so accustomed to diluting the Holy of Holies down to the level of a cuddly grandfather. We have become so comfortable and familiar with this construct we've created—that of a friendly, approachable, always accessible God—that we risk stripping

away His holiness altogether and forgetting who we're actually talking to.

Moses could not mistake the holiness of the God who spoke to him through the bush of blazing fire. "Do not come closer," God warned him in Exodus 3:5. "Remove the sandals from your feet, for the place where you are standing is holy ground." All throughout the Old Testament, the presence of God was synonymous with all things holy. A holiness that inspired fear and trembling and even the risk of death to those that dared look upon His face (Exodus 33:20). In the fire on the mountaintop, the temple, and the tabernacle, there was always a boundary that existed between God and His people. A chasm between the sinless and the sinful that simply could not be crossed.

That is until Jesus, whose dying breath on the cross ripped the temple curtain in two, crossing the divide and creating access to God "by a new and living way" (Hebrews 10:20). This allowed us to enter into His presence with a boldness that had never been possible before.

In that very moment, our relationship with God changed forever—but His holiness did not. For this is the unchanging God of Israel, whose majestic displays of awe-inspiring glory caused His people to tremble before Him. As we enter into the Holy presence of God today, we are called to do the same. To come before Him with humble, reverent hearts, and a desire to worship all that He is, "in the splendor of His holiness" (Psalm 96:9).

Lord, Thank You for this simple yet powerful reminder that You are holy. Help us enter into Your presence with a heart of worship and an attitude of reverent fear, acknowledging who You are in everything we say and do. Amen.

Written by Vicki J. Bentley

Day One

What does it mean to be holy?

Today I praise God for...

Today I am confessing...

Today I am praying for...

My reflections...

Day Two

Is holiness an attribute you regularly associate with God?

Today I praise God for...

Today I am confessing...

Today I am praying for...

My reflections...

Day Three

What is your attitude towards God when you pray?

_____

_____

_____

Today I praise God for...

_____

_____

Today I am confessing...

_____

_____

Today I am praying for...

_____

_____

My reflections...

_____

_____

Day Four

How does reading about God in the Old Testament help you have a greater understanding of His holiness today?

Today I praise God for...

Today I am confessing...

Today I am praying for...

My reflections...

Day Five

How did Jesus' ultimate sacrifice change humanity's relationship with God?

_____

_____

_____

Today I praise God for...

_____

_____

Today I am confessing...

_____

_____

Today I am praying for...

_____

_____

My reflections...

_____

_____

Day Six

How can we relate to God more intimately and directly while still acknowledging His holiness?

Today I praise God for...

Today I am confessing...

Today I am praying for...

My reflections...

Day Seven

How might regular reflection and meditation on God's holiness impact your current prayer life?

Today I praise God for...

Today I am confessing...

Today I am praying for...

My reflections...

But I tell you, love your enemies and pray for those who persecute you, so that you may be sons of your Father in heaven.

Matthew 5:44

Week 22

When You Are Disappointed in the Outcome

Trust in the Lord with all your heart, and do not rely on your own understanding; think about Him in all your ways, and He will guide you on the right paths.
Proverbs 3:5-6

Have you ever been disillusioned when your prayers felt unnoticed and unanswered? The times when God could have answered your way, but He didn't, and it made no sense at all. When you are disappointed in the outcome, does it put your faith on shaky ground? After all, we believe in a God of miracles, and He didn't give us one. Some of us will stomp our feet and run from God. Let our anger stir and fester up in bitterness. If we are not careful, this approach will drive us into unbelief.

However, we can adopt a different method. We can choose to trust in God and head straight to Him in prayer. After all, when did faith or trust depend on God delivering what we want? Honestly, I have done it both ways. How about you? All too often, I find myself with hands clenched tight, and a mind struggling to make sense of something I

can'tunderstand. "For My thoughts are not your thoughts, and your ways are not My ways." This is the Lord's declaration. "For as heaven is higher than earth, so My ways are higher than your ways, and My thoughts than your thoughts." (Isaiah 55:8-9)

However, in these times of disappointing outcomes, we merely need to remember we have already made the choice to put our trust in God. So once again, we must practice placing it all at the foot of the cross and letting it go.

Of course, it doesn't wash away the pain nor free us of unwanted circumstances. But remember, we have a God who is trustworthy; He loves us, and will never leave us. Trusting Him will help us persevere through life's challenges with a peace that makes no sense.

So when those unexpected circumstances seem to roll in one right after the other, try saying aloud, "I don't like this God. But if this is what it takes for your will to be done, I am all in. I Trust You, God."

For we walk by faith, not by sight. (2 Corinthians 5:7)

We won't always understand His ways, after all, He is God, and we are not. However, choosing to anchor to God and put our trust in Him will always be the right choice even when you are disappointed with the outcome. Because after all, how can we trust if it is contingent on the result?

Lord, Thank You for never leaving me alone in my disappointment. Forgive me for the times I fail to put my trust in You. Today, Lord, I declare, I trust in You. I know You love me, and Your plan is good and right. Guide me on this path when I can't understand Your ways. Amen

Written by Maree Dee

Day One

Have you put your trust entirely in God? List the areas you might need to relinquish.

Today I praise God for...

Today I am confessing...

Today I am praying for...

My reflections...

Day Two

Write out Proverbs 3:5-6. Do you trust God with your entire heart?

Today I praise God for...

Today I am confessing...

Today I am praying for...

My reflections...

263

Day Three

How has God shown up for you in the past? Start with "I will remember" and write out all the times you can think of where God has been faithful.

Today I praise God for...

Today I am confessing...

Today I am praying for...

My reflections...

Day Four

Spend some time meditating on Isaiah 55:8-9. Is there something new you see?

Today I praise God for...

Today I am confessing...

Today I am praying for...

My reflections...

Day Five

Spend some time in prayer, asking God to reveal to you where you need to trust Him and write that down.

Today I praise God for...

Today I am confessing...

Today I am praying for...

My reflections...

Day Six

Write out 2 Corinthians 5:7 and post it in a prominent place. How does this speak to you?

Today I praise God for...

Today I am confessing...

Today I am praying for...

My reflections...

Day Seven

What steps will you take to continue trusting God when you are disappointed in the outcome?

Today I praise God for...

Today I am confessing...

Today I am praying for...

My reflections...

Subscribe to our email list for
more daily devotions at
devotableapp.com/subscribe

I call on You, God, because You will answer me; listen closely to me; hear what I say.
                    Psalm 17:6

Week 23

A Pattern for Prayer When the Road Is Hard

And now, Lord, consider their threats, and grant that Your slaves may speak Your message with complete boldness, while You stretch out Your hand for healing, signs, and wonders to be performed through the name of Your holy Servant Jesus
Acts 4:29-30

Acts 4 paints a picture of both opposition and grace. In it, we see Peter and John miraculously heal a lame man. Soon after they are arrested and upon their trial, they defend the Gospel of Christ. While we see the Lord give Peter and John the words to speak, we do not see Him remove their opposition. In His sovereignty, the Lord sees fit to allow them to suffer persecution and meets them in it.

In the verses above, Peter and John were reunited with their frightened band of believers. Despite the high priest's threat against them, they are sure of their purpose and of their God. As they considered the road before them, they joined together and prayed an astonishing

prayer. First, they remember who God is: the Master and Creator of allthings. Second, they remember God's promise that persecution would come. In fact, they recall it was God's will that Christ would suffer. Finally, they request that God take note of their persecution and grant them boldness to continue speaking and healing in His name.

As I read this I wondered what kind of prayer I would have prayed in that moment. Would I have asked the Lord for boldness to walk the difficult road before me? Or would I have asked for an altogether different road? So often, our prayers focus on the road ahead to be easier, for God to remove the stumbling blocks, for alternate pathways. But the prayer here is not asking the Lord to change the state of things around them. It is asking the Lord to change the state of their hearts.

Are you or someone you love walking through a difficult season right now? If so, may this prayer encourage to you to cry out, not for an easier road, but for an emboldened heart. There is no shame in asking the Lord to change your circumstances; Christ did. But just as Christ, we must ultimately pray that His will be done and our hearts prepared.

Father God, You know the difficulties we are facing today. Your Word reminds us it is an honor to be persecuted in Your name, and if we share in Christ's suffering we will also share in His glory. Help us to endure our difficult circumstances with patience and compassion for our accusers. Embolden our hearts. Strengthen our faith. Fill us with Your Spirit and give us the grace to do what You have called us to. Amen.

Written by Mary Kathryn Tiller

Day One

What is your response when life gets hard?

Today I praise God for...

Today I am confessing...

Today I am praying for...

My reflections...

Day Two

Can you recall a time when God moved in your circumstance as
only the almighty God could?

Today I praise God for...

Today I am confessing...

Today I am praying for...

My reflections...

Day Three

In the space below, reflect on who you know God to be and what great things you have seen Him do in your life.

Today I praise God for...

Today I am confessing...

Today I am praying for...

My reflections...

Day Four

What promises has God given you to hold on to during times of hardship?

Today I praise God for...

Today I am confessing...

Today I am praying for...

My reflections...

Day Five

How can Jesus' example in suffering encourage you to continue on in grace?

_____

_____

_____

Today I praise God for...

_____

_____

Today I am confessing...

_____

_____

Today I am praying for...

_____

_____

My reflections...

_____

_____

Day Six

If you are walking through a difficult season today, cry out to God and believe that He is your defender and will bring you peace in due time. Write out your prayer.

Today I praise God for...

Today I am confessing...

Today I am praying for...

My reflections...

Day Seven

Ask the Lord to encourage and equip you for the road ahead.

Today I praise God for...

Today I am confessing...

Today I am praying for...

My reflections...

If you then, who are evil, know how to give good gifts to your children, how much more will your Father in heaven give good things to those who ask Him!
Matthew 7:11

Week 24

Praying for Closed Doors

Write to the angel of the church in Philadelphia: "The Holy One, the True One, the One who has the key of David, who opens and no one will close, and closes and no one opens, says: I know your works. Because you have limited strength, have kept My word, and have not denied My name, look, I have placed before you an open door that no one is able to close.
Revelation 3:7-8

      Life seems to be a series of doors, some wide open, some slightly ajar, and some locked tight. As we think and pray about the possible opportunities that are on the other side of these doors, let's consider how we have traditionally presented our requests to God. Blessings. Favor. Overflow. These words are often the theme of our prayers for ourselves and others. We believe God would withhold no good thing from us, and we cash in on that promise as much as we can. It's comfortable, and it feels good to receive an affirmative answer to our prayers. "Open the floodgates of heaven!" we proclaim, fully expecting God's outpouring that we may not have room enough to receive. That's

the stuff testimonies are made of!

However, shouldn't we trust God enough to pray for a closed door shielding us from something that isn't for our good? Absolutely. But I don't know many people who pray for closed doors. Sometimes fear, anxiety, and goals get in the way. Often, closed doors are usually associated with prayers that God has said no to. Friends, I submit that closed doors are just as important as open ones.

Let's consider God's "no" or closed door, as a "yes" - a yes to something other than what we may have our hearts set on. A yes to a different job, relationship, or location. Even a yes to that very thing we desire now, just at a later date. Prayer is our lifeline, and regardless of how we feel about the answer, we can be sure that God's heart toward us won't change.

God can be trusted to answer our prayers because He loves us. He answers with a divine wisdom and foresight we cannot fully comprehend. Friends, I want to experience both God's provision and protection in His answers to my prayers, and I hope you do too. We can experience this and more as we pray for both open AND closed doors.

Lord, thank You for being such a good Father. One that loves His children enough to say no, and close doors for our protection and provision. Help us trust You enough to watch and wait for Your good plan. Please, God, keep us focused on You, the Giver of the gifts rather than the gifts we so desperately desire. In Jesus' name we pray, Amen.

Written by Quantrilla Ard

Day One

What doors have you asked God to open for you?

_____

_____

_____

Today I praise God for...

_____

_____

Today I am confessing...

_____

_____

Today I am praying for...

_____

_____

My reflections...

_____

_____

Day Two

What impact did the open doors you prayed for have in your life?

Today I praise God for...

Today I am confessing...

Today I am praying for...

My reflections...

Day Three

Have you prayed for closed doors in your life? Why or why not?

_____

_____

_____

Today I praise God for...

_____

_____

Today I am confessing...

_____

_____

Today I am praying for...

_____

_____

My reflections...

_____

_____

Day Four

Has there been a time when God didn't answer your prayers the way you hoped He would?

_____

_____

Today I praise God for...

_____

_____

Today I am confessing...

_____

_____

Today I am praying for...

_____

_____

My reflections...

_____

_____

Day Five

How would you encourage someone who prayed for an open door
but had one closed instead?

Today I praise God for...

Today I am confessing...

Today I am praying for...

My reflections...

Day Six

Which are you more thankful for? Doors opened or doors closed? Why?

Today I praise God for...

Today I am confessing...

Today I am praying for...

My reflections...

Day Seven

What do you hope to learn/gain as God opens and closes doors in your life?

Today I praise God for...

Today I am confessing...

Today I am praying for...

My reflections...

Listen to all of our devotions
on our podcast at
devotableapp.com/podcast

If you then, who are evil, know how to give good gifts to your children, how much more will the heavenly Father give the Holy Spirit to those who ask Him?"
Luke 11:13

Week 25

The Proper Mindset for Praying

But when you pray, go into your private room, shut your door, and pray to your Father who is in secret. And your Father who sees in secret will reward you.
Matthew 6:6

Approaching God with the proper mindset is crucial. A point often overlooked is that prayer's main spotlight should be on God. When Christ's disciples asked Him how to pray, He began with a warning on approaching God with a wrong mindset. Our Messiah told His disciples that a prayer for gaining attention isn't favorable with God. Jesus said this, "Whenever you pray, you must not be like the hypocrites, because they love to pray standing in the synagogues and on the street corners to be seen by people. I assure you: They've got their reward!" (Matthew 6:5).

God opposes pride. In fact, it's the reason God removed Satan from His kingdom (Isaiah 14:12-14). Pride offends our Father because it glorifies oneself and disregards God. Pride destroys prayers because it lacks humility. And humbling myself before God shows Him my gratitude for saving me.

Now that we can see the significance in humbling ourselves before God, it's time to spend quality time with our Savior. And this means setting aside time free from distractions. It's easy for me to let personal obligations take me away from private time with the Lord. Often, I use excuses that prevent me from spending one-on-one time with God. And the results are not as effective.

When I'm alone with Him, my mind, my heart, and spirit are His. This leads to answered prayers because I'm letting Him control my life. With Christ in my life nothing can overtake my consciousness of His presence, and the rewards are astonishing.

Another obstacle when praying is repetitive phrases and long worded petitions. With this in mind, brief communication with Him opens the door to His infinite wisdom. Jesus taught this, When you pray, don't babble like the idolaters, since they imagine they'll be heard for their many words." (Matthew 6:7)

Before praying today, focus on a proper mindset. That is the key! *God, do with me as You will. I ask this in Christ's name, Amen.*

Written by Walter Kahler

Day One

What do you expect from God? Is this a realistic expectation?

_____

_____

_____

Today I praise God for...

_____

_____

Today I am confessing...

_____

_____

Today I am praying for...

_____

_____

My reflections...

_____

_____

Day Two

Do you have reservations about prayer? Why?

Today I praise God for...

Today I am confessing...

Today I am praying for...

My reflections...

Day Three

Do you set aside private time for God? How could you change your schedule to have more time with Him?

_____

_____

_____

Today I praise God for...

_____

_____

Today I am confessing...

_____

_____

Today I am praying for...

_____

_____

My reflections...

_____

_____

Day Four

Do you find yourself distracted when praying? How can you solve this issue?

_____

_____

_____

Today I praise God for...

_____

_____

Today I am confessing...

_____

_____

Today I am praying for...

_____

_____

My reflections...

_____

_____

Day Five

Are your prayers repetitive? If so, what are some things you can do to stop the repetition?

_____

_____

_____

Today I praise God for...

_____

_____

Today I am confessing...

_____

_____

Today I am praying for...

_____

_____

My reflections...

_____

_____

Day Six

Are you giving God control of your life and prayers?

Today I praise God for...

Today I am confessing...

Today I am praying for...

My reflections...

Day Seven

Are my prayers selfless or selfish?

Today I praise God for...

Today I am confessing...

Today I am praying for...

My reflections...

The Lord is near all who call out to Him, all who call out to Him with integrity.

Psalm 145:18

Week 26

Abiding Through Prayer

Abide in me, and I in you. As the branch cannot bear fruit by itself, unless it abides in the vine, neither can you, unless you abide in me.
John 15:4 (ESV)

The word abide that Jesus used in John 15:4 is a verb and therefore should prompt us to act. But what exactly are we to act on? What activity does Jesus want us to take part in so we experience this life of abidance? If we trace the root word of abide back to the original Greek through Strong's Concordance, we gain a deeper understanding. Here are a few descriptive translations: remain, dwell, continue, tarry, endure, sojourn, continue to be present, await.

These descriptors help us understand what abiding looks like, but let's challenge ourselves further by pondering how we can apply this action to our everyday, ordinary life. The apostle Paul provides us with one application of abiding in Colossians 4:2 (ESV), which reads, "Continue steadfastly in prayer, being watchful in it with thanksgiving." Continuing in prayer—or in conversation with God—is a form of abiding.

Take action by continuing steadfastly in prayer. Be watchful of the distractions that will come (your phone, the dog barking at the Amazon delivery that just came, your child that got up way before they were supposed to...it's endless). Practice gratitude and have a thankful heart. Each time you choose to tarry in the Lord's presence, remain in His Word, and await His Words as you talk with Him...you will bear fruit.

God, you offered me eternal abidance in You through Your Son, Jesus. Help me to want to abide in Your presence and be fully connected to Your Vine. I cannot do this alone. My actions are empty without Your enabling power. I choose to be a sojourner for Christ so You may be glorified. Amen.

Written by Tiffany Haynes

Day One

Read John 15:1-11. What are these verses speaking to you?

_____

_____

_____

Today I praise God for...

_____

_____

Today I am confessing...

_____

_____

Today I am praying for...

_____

_____

My reflections...

_____

_____

Day Two

What are other Biblical examples of abiding?

Today I praise God for...

Today I am confessing...

Today I am praying for...

My reflections...

Day Three

What's one way you can practice prayer more?

Today I praise God for...

Today I am confessing...

Today I am praying for...

My reflections...

Day Four

What opportunities do you have to insert conversations with God in your routine?

_____

_____

Today I praise God for...

_____

_____

Today I am confessing...

_____

_____

Today I am praying for...

_____

_____

My reflections...

_____

_____

Day Five

Do you start your day with the Word? How can you be present in His presence?

Today I praise God for...

Today I am confessing...

Today I am praying for...

My reflections...

Day Six

What distractions are you permitting into your life that are affecting your walk with God?

_____

_____

Today I praise God for...

_____

Today I am confessing...

_____

Today I am praying for...

_____

My reflections...

_____

Day Seven

Spend a few moments practicing gratitude and thanksgiving. What do you want to praise Him for today?

Today I praise God for...

Today I am confessing...

Today I am praying for...

My reflections...

Read and discover more free
devotions at devotableapp.com

Now the end of all things is near; therefore, be serious and disciplined for prayer.

1 Peter 4:7

A Special Thanks to All Devotable Authors

A couple of years ago, I had an idea to create a mobile application and website that would help me, and others, deepen our connection with God. I started that project and quickly realized I would need to partner with many talented writers, authors, and bloggers in order to make this successful.

So I started reaching out to amazing writers online and asking them to write for me, without compensation and out of the goodness of their hearts. I quickly realized there were hundreds of talented writers willing to do this, all for nothing in return.

Their passion for spreading the gospel of Christ, encouraging fellow believers, and providing astounding devotions each day has simply amazed me.

To the 100+ writers that contribute to Devotable each week, selflessly writing with the great commission as their only goal, thank you! From the bottom of my heart, thank you for all you do!

You will never know the full extent of how your writing is impacting lives on this side of heaven. Only when you get to heaven will you be able to see the impact your words have had on this world, and I know God will be waiting there to tell you, "Well done, good and faithful servant."

But until we get there, I hope my gratitude will suffice. This project wouldn't exist without you. Keep the faith, brothers and sisters!

About the Authors

Alexis M. Newlin

Alexis M. Newlin is a 36 year old lover of Jesus, loose leaf tea, roller coasters, writing stories, and going on adventures. She enjoys encouraging others by reminding them not to look at what they see, but to always look to God, Who is working in the unseen.

www.apeachincali.com

Chanel Moore

Chanel Moore is a teacher who enjoys writing. She recently finished writing her book D.A.U.G.H.T.E.R.S., focusing on what it means to be God's daughter. She also does a one-minute Bible study called Study this Book.

Instagram: @nellyacc, @studythisbook, or @daughterstogether

Chuck Kralik

Chuck Kralik is a pastor and Christian author. He loves spending time with family and friends and cheering for the Nebraska Cornhuskers!

https://chuckkralikauthor.com

Corbin Charles Henderson

Corbin Charles Henderson is a Student Pastor at First Baptist Church Ash Grove and a student at Midwestern Baptist Theological Seminary. He has been married to his wife Heaven Henderson for a little over six months and is passionate about discipleship and training future ministers of the Gospel.

Twitter: @cchenders40

Crystal A. Dixon

Crystal A. Dixon is a Bible teacher, speaker and author. Through biblical truths and application, she encourages others to seek and nurture a relationship with Jesus Christ and cultivate a lifestyle of prayer. In her spare time, Crystal loves being with her husband, Donald and their family, reading, and trips to the beach.

http://morningblessings.net/

Donna E. Lane

Donna E. Lane, Ph.D. a professor, Christian counselor, and author of Christian fiction and nonfiction. Her nonfiction titles include Strength in Adversity, Strength in Our Story, Wilderness Meditations, and more. Her fiction titles include The Interview, Sky Light Falls: Whisperers Book One, and Sky Light Rises: Whisperers Book Two.

http://donnaanddavidlane.com

Fiona "Fee" Williams

Fiona "Fee" Williams is a songwriter and blogger based out of Tampa, FL. She loves writing and encouraging believers young and old through her music and writing. Fee is a married mom of three who loves God and helping others experience the joy that comes with believing, loving, and serving Jesus Christ.

Instagram: @fionachanelwilliams

Gwen Thielges

Gwen Thielges is an author, blogger, church worship leader, and Kindermusik educator. She is married to Darren, and they have been blessed abundantly with three sons, one daughter, two daughters-in-law, and two grandsons. She enjoys photography, songwriting, and encouraging her readers to strive toward a deeper faith and a wider witness.

https://gwenthielges.com/

J. Heaven Henderson

J. Heaven Henderson is a Biblical Counselor in Ash Grove, Missouri. She is currently pursuing her ACBC certification and MA in Biblical Counseling at Baptist Bible College and Theological Seminary. Heaven serves her home church alongside her husband Corbin Henderson.

Twitter: @JillianHeaven

Jake Doberenz

Jake Doberenz wears many hats, including blogger, writer, and college-age minster. He is currently working on his Master of Theological Studies at Oklahoma Christian University. In addition to several published devotionals and articles, Jake has also published two short plays.

https://www.jakedoberenz.com

Kaysian Gordon

Kaysian Gordon is a mother, author, blogger, speaker, and Bible teacher. After years of education in the financial arena, Kaysian felt the call to start writing a faith blog. She teaches her church's youth class and speaks to various women's groups.

www.kaysigordon.com

Lauren Sparks

Lauren Sparks is a wife and mom to two daughters – one with special needs – and one bonus son. She lives, worships Jesus, and teaches yoga in the Dallas, Texas area. She is a contributing writer for *Perseverance: 30 Devotions for Faith that Moves Mountains*, and shares her adventures, victories, and flub-ups weekly on her blog.

https://laurensparks.net

Lesley Crawford

Lesley Crawford lives in Scotland and works for a Christian charity. She loves to encourage people in exploring the Bible and to help them see there is always hope to be found in Jesus, whatever circumstances they may face.

http://lifeinthespaciousplace.wordpress.com

Marilyn Nutter

Marilyn Nutter, from Greer, SC, is a contributor to magazines, on-line sites, and compilations. She is a Bible teacher and speaker for women's and grief support groups and serves on the women's ministry team at her church. In her life's seasons, she has met God's faithfulness and clings to Lam. 3:22-23.

www.marilynnutter.com

Matthew Spear

Matthew Spear is currently the student ministries pastor at Chicago First Church of the Nazarene and is working on earning his MDiv at Garrett-Evangelical Seminary.

https://oneseven.home.blog

Pamela Keener

Pamela Keener lives nestled in a tiny Colorado town close to the mountains. She proudly proclaims herself as a Jesus follower, blessed wife of 21+ years, and a momma to 6 wonderful kids! With a passion for inspiring and encouraging women to seek Jesus in their daily lives, she radiates the love and grace of God in both her writing and speaking ventures.

www.inspiredgraceforwomen.com

Quentin G. Love

Quentin G. Love is the author of TXTS FROM THE TXT, a daily devotional inspired by believers living in an increasingly more mobile, tech-centered world. All of the devotions and prayers are originally started as a morning text message amongst friends, family, and fellow followers of Christ.

www.quentinglove.com

Sarah Geringer

Sarah Geringer is a speaker, artist, and author of Transforming Your Thought Life: Christian Meditation in Focus. When she's not reading over 100 books per year, Sarah enjoys painting, baking, gardening, and playing the flute. She lives in her beloved home state of Missouri with her husband and three children.

https://www.sarahgeringer.com

Stephanie Caesara

Stephanie Caesara is an Indonesian woman who is passionate to share her story with Jesus and reach the lost. She desires to help women find their true identity and bring them to their true calling in Christ.

Instagram: @victorious.women

Trip Kimball

Trip Kimball is a pastor–missionary who focuses on discipleship and leadership development. He is part of a group of experienced pastors who coach, mentor, assess, and help with pastoral transitions. He has written a book and many training materials, and regularly writes online and on his blog.
www.word-strong.com/contact

Vicki J. Bentley

Vicki J. Bentley lives in Upstate New York with her husband and two young daughters. Through her devotional writings and articles, she encourages Christians to pursue Jesus-centered, joy-filled living in the trenches of adulthood and parenthood.
https://purposefuljoy.wordpress.com/

Maree Dee

Maree Dee is a Writer | Speaker | Advocate | Ministry Leader - passionate about encouraging and equipping others to embrace life in the midst of the unexpected. She is a warrior who doesn't give up when the journey gets tough. Maree believes, together with God, we can all find incredible joy along the way, even when surrounded by tremendous pain.
https://www.mareedee.com

Mary Kathryn Tiller

Mary Kathryn Tiller is a freelance writer and blogger based in rural East Texas. As a mother, small business owner, and self-proclaimed theology nerd, she has spent the last five years asking the question, "How exactly does today's modern woman live her life as Christ?" Through her blog, she shares her struggles and insights, leading women to cultivate a faithful heart in a frenzied world.

https://marykathryntiller.com

Quantrilla Ard

Quantrilla Ard is a faith-based personal and spiritual development writer who lives in the DC Metro area with her husband and three littles. In addition to being a dedicated wife and mother, she is an entrepreneur, doctoral student, and curator of all things lovely.

https://thephdmamma.com

Walter Kahler

Walter Kahler loves sharing Christ's impact on his life. Nothing brings him more joy than expressing God's message of salvation!

www.achristianmindset.org

Tiffany Haynes

Tiffany Haynes is the founder and creator of Divinely Interrupted, a blog that encourages ordinary women to study God's extraordinary Word and live surrendered. Tiffany takes the Word of God and provides simple, verse-by-verse commentary coupled with relevant application. You become less and Jesus becomes more.

https://www.divinelyinterrupted.com/

Made in the USA
Las Vegas, NV
19 December 2020